T0159041

GROWING

UP•
Grifton

A Collection of Stories About a Man and His Town

GEORGE SUGG AND DIANE THOMAS

authorHOUSE®

AuthorHouse™
1663 Liberty Drive
Bloomington, IN 47403
www.authorhouse.com
Phone: 1 (800) 839-8640

Published by AuthorHouse 11/07/2018

ISBN: 978-1-5462-6753-9 (sc)
ISBN: 978-1-5462-6752-2 (e)

Print information available on the last page.

This book is printed on acid-free paper.

DEDICATION

I dedicate

Growing Up Grifton

to my beloved great grandson

Grady Blaine Bright.

He is three years old.

He keeps me going.

George Sugg

FOREWORD

I am in the generation below George and a deeply rooted Grifton girl. For all my life I have known who George was but our paths rarely crossed. He knew me to be a writer and wanted help with a story he was working on about Grifton. I obliged out of respect. Nothing more.

That first story intrigued me. He asked me to help with another. Told me he wanted to write about our town and could really use my help. I was not about to commit long term to such a task but continued to help him. I was fascinated with his knowledge and memory of our area. He was writing about history that touched me. These were people and places I had enjoyed but took for granted all of my life. I was deeply hooked. After a few more stories I told him that he was writing a book and pushed him for the next installment. I was not only committed by this time but eager for each next story. Honored that I got to help bring them to life.

The tales contained in this little book are like so many small towns across America. This telling is of Grifton though. Growing Up Grifton is the history of how this town grew to be a thriving and important community and some of those who made it happen. It is the memories of the boy who grew up with her. George also became a vital part of the place. Refusing to take the stories with him when he goes. I am proud to be a part of the telling.

I live is Alaska now. It is where life recently took me. I return to Grifton often. I still have a house there. My heart still beats for that little eastern North Carolina town by the banks of the Contentnea Creek. It is rich in important history. Some of the history is recorded on these pages so that others may know and remember her as well.

Diane Mitchell Thomas

PREFACE

I moved away from Grifton when I retired. The fishing, hunting, and golf of Belhaven lured me to the coast. My heart never left my small hometown though. It shaped my life and has always been a part of me. I think of her, the people and that way of life almost daily. Times are different now. I wish others could experience the rich heritage of small town living as I knew it.

This book was written to record some of that history. So few are alive to know it now. A graveyard is full of untold stories that will never be heard. I didn't want to take mine with me. I hope every reader of my stories will feel enriched for picking up this little book. Better know how Grifton grew. How I grew up with her.

This would not have happened without Diane. She willingly shared her writing skills to help make the stories more readable. I appreciate her generous help. Together we hope this collection from my memory will help keep our heritage alive. I hope we will find our way back to some of the best of small town living. Maybe we will find our way back to Grifton.

George Sugg

THE COLLECTION

Chapter One

GRIFTON DOWNTOWN

I am a man in my nineties now. I can still see it clearly if I close my eyes to remember those days. Just as it was. I can almost smell the aroma of the peanuts roasting down the street. The scent of tobacco as men gathered on the sidewalk in a huddle. Smoking. Talking. Laughing. The women greeting each other and glad for the break from the hard work at home. Children running up and down the sidewalk in play as they meet their friends. I watched the little town of Grifton grow over the years as it grew me to manhood in return. I felt the need to pen my memories. So that when I am gone those that come after me will have the story of her beginning. It had been such a place of prosper. I hope the pages of this book will allow the reader to come back with me in time to know her and the countless other small towns like her across America.

Most vivid are the years between 1935 and up until 1960. The population during most of this time was only between four and five hundred. The street was lined with stores and shops that did a constant and brisk business for such a small place. It mostly thrived on the people who lived outside the township. The farming families. Grifton was a farming community. The land out of town was full of small acreage farmers who sought supplies to sustain their way of living. A few owned their land while many were tenant farmers and relied on sharecropping. Tobacco was the main livelihood. The government controlled the growth and each were given an allotment. The crops of soy bean and cotton helped make ends meet. Chickens were raised for eggs and sustaining food. You could even buy the chicks in town. Grifton offered everything the residents of the area needed.

Farmers had accounts at the feed and grain store or one of the many general stores that sold a little of almost everything it seemed to me. J.R. Harvey sold baby clothing, fine millinery, and even coffins. There were three service stations and as many grocery stores. Two drug stores were just doors apart. The fish market offered bins of iced and smelly fish. You could shop at the local clothing stores or browse the five and dime. The town had doctor's offices, a shoe repair store, and a bank. Some still drove a mule and cart in from the countryside and the two livery stables were there to help. A cotton mill stood in town as well. Mouthwatering hot dogs and hamburgers did not cost much and came fresh from the grill and wrapped in thin paper. It was difficult to choose between that or the cost of the ticket at the movie theatre just down the street. The home town had it all.

Nearly all the stores had a tin canopy over their front doors that protruded out and over the sidewalks. Wooden benches lined the streets and welcomed the shopper to sit and visit his neighbor. An artesian well flowed freely in front of the bank and was a favorite spot for all on a hot summer day. It disappeared when the DuPont plant came to the area. The manufacturer drew so much water that the well eventually dried up. Only God knows the number of people that drank water from that well. It was cool, refreshing, and good for satisfying a thirsty mouth. Many today still remember it. There are more who cannot even imagine it.

The town was busy all week long but it was each Saturday that it really took on another life. It was astounding to see such a number of people come into town. The atmosphere almost felt like a circus. The farm work ceased for the week and they came from all the outlying areas to get supplies and socialize. They cleaned up and wore the best clothes they had. They dressed for town. I am not sure why but they did. Entire families would load into their cars for the trip into Grifton. There were not so many pickup trucks back then. Every parking space that lined the streets were full. Some stores had a place to tie your mule or horse. The town had only one policemen in those days. More was not needed. He did not even own a uniform. I never saw a problem. Just friendliness and respect. Regardless of color, gender, or socio standing.

Attention to customer was prime in that day. It took longer without the modern electronics that merchants depend on these days. I worked in Roy Jackson's grocery store and once with H.P Quinerly. He had a soda fountain in his store. I recall there were no shopping carts because one did not need to load their own groceries. The customer came to the counter with his long list and called them off to the clerk in attention. He would run and get each item called and place it on a table. A running tally of the purchases were recorded on a brown paper bag with a pencil. The clerk did all the running. The bill would be added using your head and the listing on the bag. A total was then rung up on a mechanical cash register. It was a slow process but the customers in line seemed patient as they enjoyed their time in town and break from their usual routine on the farm.

I was forever looking for a way to prosper along with the town. Mack Dixon was always busy in his barbershop. He had a shoeshine booth in there that he did not have time for. Since people were in their best clothes I believed clean shoes was a waiting market. I had watched Mack and observed him closely. I made a mental note of what was needed to shine shoes and began making purchases to stock my own box. I finally had all I needed and walked the downtown streets offering my services. The cost was ten cents. People did want their shoes shined and it was a big success. Sometimes they would flip me a quarter. I remembered those folks that tipped and always gave them a little extra the next time. Each Saturday afternoon I would go home and count my coins. I thought that maybe I was rich.

That is how the town was when it was growing. I was indeed rich just to be raised there. It was so alive. That is not her fate now. Most of those stores are gone. The buildings disappeared or are vacant. The small farms do not exist anymore. Their farmhouses have fallen into disrepair or vanished completely. Easy transportation have taken the shoppers to the larger towns nearby. The pages in this book are a recording of how it happened. Perhaps a map of sorts. To show us a path back. Walk with me as I remember. Let's walk slowly. To cherish.

Chapter Two

THE COBB HOTEL

It was a gem for our small town. A cream colored hotel that boast lots of gingerbread trim and a turreted porch over its second story. The Cobb Hotel was built in the year 1900 by a woman named, Alice Spear, from nearby Greenville. It was located on Main Street where many of the town's affluent built their homes. You would reach it by going south on Church Street and turn left on Main. It was the third building on the left and was quite the landmark of its day. That was the street that was also closer to the creek where the steamboats docked and was a short walk to the train depot in the opposite direction. The hotel was centrally located to the chosen mode of transportation and convenient for travelers who came to Grifton.

The town bustled with activity in those years. Drummers, or salesmen, flooded Grifton as they pedaled their wares to the many stores there. Automobiles had not come out at this time and they rented horse and buggy or simply chose to walk the streets on foot. Quail was plentiful in eastern North Carolina and many hunters from the north came in search of a good shoot. The Cobb Hotel was where they rested and did so in comfort and style.

It was modern for its day with large windows sufficient for air flow in the hot summer months. Each room had a lovely fireplace for the colder winter days. The building was made entirely of wood. Heart pine was the timber of the area and most used for building. That makes for a stunning sight on a floor but as it ages it turns to lightwood which is extremely flammable. If it meets fire it quickly becomes an inferno. Most kitchens were built at the back of a house for that reason. The hotel kitchen was located at the rear as well to keep it as isolated from the rest of the house as possible.

The introduction of automobiles and the more building of hotels in nearby towns caused a decline in the use of that fine hostelry in our little town. The railroads had four trains a day by this time, two freight and two passengers, that came through and showed a margin of fifteen hundred dollars in business a month. That was a lot of money for that time. It also took the drummers on and away from Grifton without need to stay overnight. The Cobb Hotel had to depend on other means for survival. The establishment began to rent out the rooms to local people who needed housing. It became an apartment building of sorts. It was quite a large place and could house several families at one time. One tenant was Ivor Cole and her family. She would be one of the last to live there.

As Grifton became a more modern town it became apparent to the mayor, Roger Johnson, and the board of aldermen that a fire department was needed. They purchased a brand new Chevrolet pumper. It was a beauty and we were quite proud of it. For some reason that I can't imagine I was appointed fire chief and was asked to organize a group of volunteers to form the first town fire department. I was very honored and rounded up some of my friends. The ones I remember were L.A. Butler, George Saleeby, Julius Chauncey, John Chapman, Wilbur and Walter Murphy and Odell Bowen. We were the department and ready when the truck arrived.

The delivery man of the new truck took us to the sand hole at nearby Edward's Bridge and spent hours showing us how to pump water from the pond to the fire hose. We were happy with our truck and did enjoy our role as firemen. Grifton even installed a water system complete with fire hydrants located at several locations around the town.

We began answering fire calls and the rush of adrenaline was exciting and difficult to explain. It was a race to see who could first reach the fire house sitting at the end of Brooks Ally because they would get to drive the truck. It would take about three miles of pushing the accelerator to the floorboard of that water filled tank just to reach fifty five miles an hour. I did once get up to sixty. One day a church caught fire just down highway 118 and we rushed to the sight. It was totally in flames. Saleeby ran to one of the windows with ax in hand and tried to smash it open. Unfortunately, the ax slipped and landed inside and burned with the church. We did not feel quite ready for so major a fire but one day that call came.

It was the Cobb Hotel on Main. Most of the department answered. It was such a short distance away but as soon as we reached it we knew the five hundred gallons of water would never be enough. We drove the truck to the corner of Church and Queen and hooked up to the hydrant there and ran the hose to the site of the fire. The pump would increase in pressure as the truck engine speed was increased. We gunned it. Chauncey was holding the hose that was pointed toward the hotel and when the pump was turned on it knocked him to the ground and he held onto that hose for dear life. It scrubbed him all over the front lawn like a caught fish but he soon was able to gain control and rise to fight the raging fire before us. Ivor's infant son, Mike, was passed out through one of the large windows and to safety. There were the scratches and bruises on Julius and we were grateful there were no other casualties that day.

Except for the Cobb herself. She was a victim of the blaze. It burned to the ground. That heart pine had made it impossible to extinguish. The town fire department is better trained today and offers good and valuable protection for the area. On that day the community was saddened at the pile of burned ashes that had been such a glorious turn of the century showpiece. Grifton had forever lost one of her jewels that day and another piece of our beautiful history had become a pile of ugly ruin. We watched the smoldering ashes of her that day and mourned the loss.

Chapter Three

COX TRAILERS

He was a visionary. Our little hometown of Grifton, and many of the families, were sustained because of that fact. His name was Leon Cox. Everyone called him Nap. He was my uncle and lived just a short walk away from our house. I lived with my grandmother while growing up. Uncle Nap had married her sister, Jessie. Both houses were on Queen Street and we visited them almost every afternoon and usually near dark.

Leon had moved to Grifton during the late 1800's. It was a farming community then. Mostly corn, soybeans, with tobacco being the main money crop of the day. Leon studied his neighbors and knew there was a need for their equipment repair. He built a large two story repair shop on the corner of Queen and Gordon Street. The shop was divided into three sections. Repair was in the front. He used the middle for a blacksmith shop. In the back was a grist mill where the farmers could take their corn to be ground into meal. The mill had two large stones facing each other and they turned to grind the corn into small bits and pieces. The stones were powered by a gasoline engine.

The blacksmith shop was fired by coal in a pit with a hand crank blower which created a very hot fire. The fire heated the metal which was then hammered into various shapes for the front shop. This was in the day before electric motors. Uncle Nap used a car motor to turn an overhead shaft. That shaft ran different tools like his drills and lathes. Electric motors did eventually replace the gasoline engine. The front shop made and sold soy bean harvesters, and the many tobacco trucks the farmers needed. Mule carts also made up the inventory and various other items that would help sustain the farmer in his fields. They were repaired at the shop when the need arose.

Leon Cox had a keen mind for design and building. Some would say he was a mechanical genius. He used his blacksmith shop and tools at hand to make or repair anything the farmers of the area needed. When we visited his home he would usually be sitting in his overstuffed chair with pencil in hand and writing figures on a brown paper bag. I was young and much later did I realize he was working on new gear ratios for the latest project for the shop. His brain never stopped. He knew that the gas motor powered overhead shaft had to have pulleys of certain sizes to turn his tools a fixed RPM. He could always work it out easily it seemed. He would figure it out on one of those brown paper bags.

I remember that he wore overalls to work each day and a funny looking cap. It was his uniform of sorts. There was a small office that had been built on the left side of his shop but he was rarely there. He was more often found out and about near his tools. Everyone liked Nap Cox. He was known to be pleasant and the farmers enjoyed their dealings with him. He could handle the repairs brought to him and his customers seemed satisfied with his charges. They knew him to be fair.

Uncle Nap fathered three sons. His namesake, Leon, and then John, were born by his first wife, Mollie. After her death, he married my Aunt Jessie. Fred was born to them. It was Fred that took an interest in the business. He had more of a business sense than his father. Nap was caught up with making things run smoothly. Fred knew the business could grow and be more profitable. It was about to be more than either could have imagined.

Fred loved to hunt and was an avid fisherman. Many boats were kept moored down at Contentnea Creek for easy fishing access. Boats could also be rented. Fred kept one there but loved fishing in other waters as well. He talked to his father about building a trailer to haul his vessel. Nap drew a plan for a simple design that would safely transport the boat. This did make it possible for Fred to take his boat to different locations to fish. Others anglers took notice and began to inquire about one for themselves. Fred saw the possibilities and Cox Trailers was about to be born.

Fred had four sons of his own. Billy, Steven, David, and Jerry, were born to Fred and his wife, Callie. Billy was mechanically inclined like his grandfather. He also remembers working in the old shop downtown as a youngster. The other three were too young to recall it. The downtown shop was not large enough or well equipped to handle the demand for the boat trailers. They had outgrown the space. Fred purchased land just north of Grifton on Highway 11. A building was erected and Cox Trailers began full production. The four boys all went away to school. Billy did return to work full time at the family owned business.

It was a huge success. The trailers were shipped all along the east coast. Boats were built larger and larger and Cox Trailers made sure they kept up and had a trailer to haul each one. It also kept food on the table for a lot of the local townsfolk. The business employed many people over the years. As high as one hundred and fifty at a time. It was quite an industry for a town so small and contributed greatly to the town of Grifton. Fred Cox was a family man and hired most of his family to work there. My wife, Edna, kept books there for many years.

The trailer business eventually expanded to include campers. That had become a favorite pastime with so many and the running gear of a camper is similar to that of a boat trailer. The land across the street was purchased and the camper assembly line began. Campers were manufactured in Grifton and delivered all across the country. Billy Cox obtained several patents for various parts used in that industry. I kept ten Cox Campers to rent out when I owned the Sport Shop in town.

The boys grew up and moved away and the business sold in 1989. The buyer proved to be an unsavory character who quickly took it under ground. It closed in 1990 and sadly sat vacant for many years. When Hurricane Floyd hit our area in 1999 the buildings became a hub of activity again. The Baptist Men came to aid in the rebuilding of the flooded town and needed a space. The old site of Cox Trailers buildings fit their need. It is now Grifton Mission Ministries and they continue to give to our town.

This is a vital story of a town's history. It is part of what made Grifton grow. Nap died of liver complications in 1951. Fred died in 2001. All four of Fred Cox's sons are living in various places and doing well.

Chapter Four

THE POTATO GRADER

Grifton was a once a thriving farming community. The local businesses in town relied on the small farmer. The yield of the earth sustained us all. Summer work in the fields brought an opportunity for young people to earn money for school clothes each year. Most worked in tobacco. It was long, hard, and dirty work. Tobacco stalks were gummy in the hot sun of the south. The pay was not bad. Money went further then. A Pepsi only cost a nickel in those days.

Local crops consisted of tobacco, corn, and cotton. Very few now remember that Irish potatoes were also once a good yield of the day. It was a vital harvest in the years between 1935 and 1945. The season was only about three weeks long. Pay was twelve and one half cents per hour. I worked it the season when I was thirteen years old. The potato grader in town was owned by W.I Bissette. We called him Mr. Ivan and he owned the Smith Douglas fertilizer company located at the corner of Queen and Gordon Streets. The grader was kept on the platform of the Grifton Depot on the side where the tracks run just next to it.

It was fun to watch the old machine grade and sort the potatoes to sizes. The Grifton grader was smaller than others. Some even had the ability to wash the produce. Ours did not. The seasonal grader work employed about fifteen people. The potatoes would be dumped into a hopper. It had motor driven screens with various size holes. The smaller potatoes would drop first. They ended up in burlap bags which were sewn together. It was my job to sew them up and help load them onto the waiting freight train cars. Three or four of us boys would stand around the machine and watch the grading process. The air was acrid with the smell of potatoes that had rotted. If not careful one would often get hit in the head with a rotten potato that was thrown out by the machine.

I made a grand total of twenty one dollars that summer. It was a lot of money for a young person at the time. It was certainly a lot of money for me. I had saved every cent. I knew what I was going to do with it. I had wanted a good camera for a long time. My parents took me to a camera store in Greenville. I eyed a 35 mm Argus. They were popular in that day. My heart was set on buying it. I asked several questions and was satisfied with my purchase. I had gotten very interested in photography and had my own dark room to develop my film.

I still have that camera. It works even though a digital one has now replaced my use of it. I pull my Argus out from time to time and remember the summer of the potato grader. I recall how I would run down the street to Smith and Douglas at the end of the week for my pay. My Ivan would always greet me with the words, "Have you been a good boy scout?" I never forgot those words or that summer. The camera helps me to remember.

Chapter Five

HART BROTHERS

The store was a town fixture. It was a general mercantile that sold everything from shoes, nails, and hoop cheese. It was located in the heart of Grifton but had its beginnings at Maple Cypress which is about six miles east of there. The brothers, Thad and Heber Hart, opened the store during the early part of the 1900's. Times became very tight and the depression was looming. There was not enough people in the surrounding area for the store to make a profit. The brothers would need to look elsewhere for their livelihood. It was time to move the business to town.

They settled on the location just a few doors down from the current Grifton Town Hall building. Most folks from middle age and up remember Hart Brothers and probably shopped from there on more than one occasion. If you shut your eyes you can almost smell the aroma of freshly roasted peanuts from the small machine located at the entrance of the store. Inside were shelves on both the left and right walls that held all sorts of merchandise. Some items were kept in glass show cases. At the very back and on the left was the office which housed a large metal safe.

It was a treat to go inside and I often went just to browse and get a whiff of those delicious peanuts. I do not remember the original owners very well but I do recall the second generation. Ed and Claude took over after their father died. Then Joseph Milton, or Jigger, as we called him. Conrad was the last owner. Their sister Ida Margaret had helped her brothers from time to time. They were all outgoing and friendly and it was a pleasure to do business there and just stop and chat as I often did.

You could purchase almost anything you needed from that one store. They sold clothes, boots, groceries, and hardware. If it was needed then the brothers had probably thought to stock it. Sometimes it seemed that they supplied things that were not desired and it might lay there for a long time. There was rarely such a thing as a discount. It just stayed there until it sold. This was not the case with the floppy hats. It looked like they were there to stay and so with great reluctance the price of them was finally reduced.

Grifton residents, Billie Mann and Jennifer Smith, were very good high school friends. They wandered into the store one afternoon to browse and pass some time. On this particular day they spotted the table of floppy hats. There were several colors available of red, blue, purple, green and yellow. They were made of felt, flopped way down in the front, and had a generous brim. There was no telling how long they had been in the store but were now priced to sell. The girls took turns trying them on and both admired the hats and ending up buying one apiece. They were quite happy with their buy and the Harts were glad to see this particular merchandise go with the girls.

Billie had a sister, Ella, who was attending East Carolina University and one day the Grifton best friends decided to visit her on campus. They had donned their newly purchased hats and it seems they were a sensational hit as they paraded around the university grounds. Several coeds stopped them to ask where they were able to find such unique hats. They told them they acquired them from a store in their home town. Hart Brothers was never known to be a chic place to shop and the girls did not want to admit that they came from what they considered to be such a lowly place. They were pressed for more information. The girls looked at each other and one spoke up and said that it came from Hart's Boutique on Queen. They felt quite smug with their answer.

It was much later that they found out that several of those coeds loaded up a car and came to Grifton for some of those floppy hats. They rode up and down the street several times looking for Hart's Boutique. They stopped in Hart Brothers store to inquire and there discovered the table of colorful hats. The store sold out of them that very afternoon. The owners were glad for the sale but did not order anymore.

The store closed down many years ago. The Hart brothers have all died and there is no smell of the peanuts when you ride through town now. The store is still remembered though and mentioned by those of us who went in and out of its door. It almost seems like yesterday.

Chapter Six

THE SPORT SHOP

The Grifton Sport Shop just evolved. It was not planned. When World War II was over the Navy placed a lot of pressure on us to stay in. The excitement of war was over for me though. I had enough. I just wanted to come home. Home was a house where the post office is now located. I had lived with my grandparents since I was eighteen months old. My parents were quite poor, my mother was expecting a baby, and my dad was gone a lot. I also think my grandparents simply wanted me with them. The house was large enough to even accommodate my aunt and uncle, Maxine and Cecil Cobb, when they married.

Joe Quinerly was a friend of mine and he came home about the same time. He had flown C47 during the war. We both joined the Civil Air Patrol and Joe taught me to fly. We did several times a week but I still longed for more than what I had in my life at the time. I was thinking about returning to school to be a veterinarian and Auburn was the school of my choice. So many people were going back after getting out of service that Auburn was crowded and I could not get in. I settled for a couple of years at East Carolina in nearby Greenville.

One day Joe told me that he thought Grifton needed a dry cleaners. Owning a business had always been a dream of mine and that idea stayed with me for a while. I had no money but talked it over with my uncle Cecil. He believed it to be a good idea, agreed to help, and we began to research that industry. It was the fifties and dry cleaning was in demand with the fabric of that day. We built a 30 X 60 cement block building and ordered all the required equipment. It was very demanding. The necessary steam for pressing kept it stifling hot and it smelled of kerosene from the cleaning fluid. The place was full of racks for storing the clothes. It also proved to be a successful venture. We made enough money to add an addition to the original building that made it twice as large. My dream had paid off.

Uncle Cecil was an avid fisherman and loved to spend time on the Contentnea Creek with his fly rod and top water baits that he made himself. They proved to be so good that people began to request and purchase them. He carved out a small section of the dry cleaners to add a bait shop. This was the beginning of the Grifton Sport Shop.

Cecil eventually retired and began raising flowers for landscaping. Edna and I were left with the business of the cleaners and the sports shop. She worked for Cox Trailers which was another local and successful business. Edna was from Lenoir County and had been raised on a farm. She was no stranger to hard work. I had fallen in love with her and married her on June 6th, 1953. It was a good move because she supported me in everything I did. I appreciated that because our days proved to be long. Retail business suited her. Our daughter, Nancy, grew up with the business and was also a valuable help to us.

The Sport Shop took up essential space of the building as the inventory of fishing items grew. We added boats, outboard motors, and eventually were selling Cox trailers and campers. New technology in fabric caused a decline in the need for dry cleaning and that part of the business was dwindling. Most of my time was demanded in the sporting side and I had a man from nearby Kinston to operate the cleaning side until it was eventually phased out completely. I devoted my full attention to the sporting goods. It was about to change in a big way.

Archery has always interested me. I had made my own bow as a kid and shot it every day except Sunday. My grandmother, Johnnie Gardner, did not allow it on that day. That was the Lord's day and when the church bell rang she believed in sitting on a pew. I did at least think about it even on a Sunday. I carried a few Fred Bear recurve bows for sale in the store. We were lucky to sell one bow a month. Burt Reynolds and the movie, Deliverance, changed all of that. Because of the focus on the bow shooting in that movie and the beginning of white tail deer season in North Carolina my business was about to really take off in ways I could not imagine.

Tommy Riley and I went hunting on the first day of the season and I shot a deer not even knowing how to dress it. The population of Grifton was about eighteen hundred at the time and I knew my sales would be limited unless I could make my prices competitive which was not an easy feat for such a small town business. One day a salesman from Bear Archery walked into the store and tried to convince me to buy a shipment of one hundred compound bows. I thought he had lost his mind but he promised to pick up any I did not sell. I agreed and they arrived on an eighteen wheeler. Those bows were so easy to shoot that women entered the hunt. In two weeks I had to call for another shipment.

I toyed with the idea of mail order and began to research it. With a catalog you could mail all over the entire country. It didn't matter if you had a fancy store because a customer in New York could not see more than the picture listed. We started a small catalog with a toll free number. The business grew to include other brand bows, clothes, and accessories. I eventually had to rent some empty stores in town for the stock I needed. It was a growing business and I could not have done it without some of the most superior help to be found anywhere. There were numerous young people right in Grifton that were smart and hard working and helped me go from a computer the size of a large piece of furniture to one that resembled a shoe box. They required little supervision and often supervised me. I owe them a debt of gratitude.

I sold the store after forty years. I was not tired of it but I wanted to fish, hunt, and play more golf. Edna and I moved to Pungo Creek to retire. The store even followed me there. One day I opened the front door to a knock. A middle aged man was standing there that I did not recognize. He introduced himself and told me that he used to come into the store when he about twelve. He told us a little about himself which was a pretty tough life partly because of some bad choices he had made. He asked if I would come to the car with him and I did. With tears in his eyes he reached into the glove compartment and pulled out a new looking Buck knife. He proceeded to tell me he had taken it from my store when he visited as a boy. The knife was stolen. It had always eaten at him and he wanted to return it. I took the knife from him and turned it over in my hand. I gave it back and told him he was free from the anguish. Keep it, I told him, to remember the torment of bad choices, and I wished him well.

The Sports Shop is gone now. From dream to memory. We had sold to customers all over the United States and several foreign countries. Most people from Grifton went into one side of the building or the other from time to time. To pick up clean clothes or get help to fish or hunt. I often regret selling when I did and wonder what it could have become if I had kept it. But it too is a memory now. A very good one.

Chapter Seven
THE FABRIC SHOP

It is still there. Much like it was. The little red wooden building on South Gordon Street. Still kept up quite well. White gingerbread corbels stand like sentinels proudly holding the front overhang. It is quiet now. It did not used to be. It was a chatterbox. Full of town talk. Occasional gossip. Where the women gathered. Full of activity it was. The town fabric shop. Whose life began elsewhere in the village. Just mere blocks away. Few now remember that early beginning.

The old Grifton Lumber Company was located just past the north end of town and behind where the present Methodist church is built on McRae. It was owned by Cecil Cobb and his onsite office building was built sturdy and of the finest lumber available. It was rusty red in color and was warmly heated by a pot belly stove. The roof was clad in tin. It was much too good to let go to ruin when the lumber company closed. Cecil owned the property on Gordon that he had purchased from the J.R. Harvey Company. It housed the dry cleaning plant we both operated. The office building was successfully moved to the south side of this business and sat in the new location with no future plans for its use.

Thomas Gardner was my uncle and a very smart business man. He was quite sought after for hire. He had graduated from North Carolina State College and majored in textiles. He well knew the business of fabric and fibers. He had first worked for the Cramerton Mills and later became vice president of Regal Corporation. They were both giant fabric maker companies. He had two sisters that still lived in Grifton. They were my mother, Joyce Sugg, and Maxine Cobb, who happened to be married to Cecil.

It was Thomas who suggested the idea of the fabric shop to his sisters. He would be their knowledgeable guide. The sisters trusted him. They eyed the empty little red building on Gordon Street until Cecil gave them permission to use it. Maxine loved to sew and Joyce loved to talk. They made a good business pair. A small addition was built onto the back to give enough room to house a good selection of the material, patterns, and all the notions required for sewing. The doors opened for business during the 1950s.

They were ready. The building was stocked almost to the ceiling with bolt after bolt of fabric. It was a kaleidoscope of color. The fresh smell of dye so strong it would sting your eyes. There was also the unmistakable odor of moth balls to protect the wool that was showcased in the shop. The town's women did not have to take the long drive to Greenville now. Fashion could be bought right in our little town. The little bell above the door signaled the many customers coming in to buy. A couple of times a year you could see a line of girls marching from the high school a few blocks away. It was the Home Economics group heading to the fabric store. They were learning to sew and would select cloth for their class project from the shop on Gordon.

The business thrived for years. Many locals were clothed their entire youth from the fabric bought in that shop. The women would hold fashion events to show off their creations. It was a highlight for many. Yards of pastel would leave the building in the spring time for the Easter frocks. It was a successful venture and continued until the 1970s. Joyce and Maxine were not young when they began the business and age had finally caught up with them. They could not deny it and felt it best to close shop and so they did.

Maxine's daughter, Jane Cobb Harris, owns the building now. She and her husband, Jerry, have kept it maintained well. It has housed other businesses over the years but none rose to the success of the Fabric Shop. It is quiet now. The shelves are empty of the colors that once graced it. The bell over the door is silent these days. The smell of fresh dye long removed. It is now just a place to reminisce about. To think of colorful frocks and be joyful of the beauty it stirred within our town.

Chapter Eight

GOWER'S STORE

There is a large and vacant lot across the creek on the Lenoir side. It is just a quiet and barren corner now. Nothing stands there at all. A far and silent cry from one hundred years ago. It sat across the creek from the town of Grifton. Right by the water's edge of the Contentnea. The store that Gower's built. There are many still alive that have their own memories of that landmark that stood for a century.

Waldo Henry Gower moved to Grifton in 1913 and married, Miss Eleanor Hanrahan Worthington, who lived about a mile out of town. The Worthington house stood near the ACL railroad tracks on land that her family farmed. Part of the land was later purchased from the Gower family for the building of the Golf Course. I saw the house many years ago but there was no road leading to it any longer. It used to be reached by an unpaved road off of Highway 11 near the horse stables at the edge of town. I do not know if any part of it still exists.

W.H. Gower was a self made entrepreneur. He first

worked at the J.R. Harvey Company in town as a salesman. He did that for many years and was quite good at it. He finally decided he did not like working for someone else and took his savings and purchased the land at the foot of the Lenoir County side of the bridge. More and more cars were being driven at that time which brought more traffic by his corner. He built his store there and thought of ways to earn a good income. It turned out that he was very good at promoting.

He sold gasoline and tires for those cars that passed each day. The store was stocked with everyday needs like groceries, fresh meats, and dry goods. Gower's store was a one stop shopping place. He obtained a monkey and kept him in a wire cage at the front of his business. Called him Monk and dressed him in a red leather collar. People were drawn to shop there just to see the mischievous monkey. W.H. was the only one who could control him. One man tried to provoke him by waving a twenty dollar bill in front of his little face. The animal was very quick, grabbed the bill, and instantly tore it to shreds as the loser could only look in stunned horror. Gower's took his unusual pet into Grifton in the cage or on a leash. They always drew a crowd.

The prize fights began soon after the store opened. Just across the highway from his store he built a boxing ring and hired some boxers. He would furnish the gloves to anyone who wanted to fight the opponents for the night. It always drew a crowd and they shopped at his store while there. He sold a lot of beer and soft drinks to those at ringside. Customers were just as drawn to his winning personality.

Everyone liked him and he treated them well and with respect.

He even opened an oyster bar there by the creek. It was long, narrow, and built parallel to the bridge. It extended about a third of the way across the water with windows for good viewing of it and the small boats of fishermen that might pass. The bar was also eye level to the bridge for view of the passing traffic. The Contentnea certainly did not grow oysters and they came from Rose Bay and other places where they could purchase them. It was always opened during the season and quite a hit with the townsfolk and beyond.

W.H. constantly gave thought to ways of making a better living. At one point he opened a fish market in downtown Grifton. They sold fish, beer, soft drinks, candy and cigarettes. It was in the area where the current auto parts store is now. I particularly remember that you could buy a single cigarette for one cent. His son, the younger Waldo, operated it for him. We called him Bud. I left for college and World War II changed life for me and so many others. I joined the Navy and so did Bud. He was on the USS Hull when it sank in the South Pacific. I do not know what happened to the fish market. I don't remember it open anymore.

Waldo lived life full and good. He purchase a thirty five foot yacht and kept it moored at the country club marina in New Bern. One day he decided to bring the vessel to Grifton. He did that very thing and kept it tied to one of the pilings of the bridge by his store. People were astonished that he could maneuver a boat that size up the narrow straits of the Contentnea. He often took his friends for a ride up and down the creek.

W. H. Gower had three children. Thomas, Waldo "Bud", and Mary Eleanor. They are all deceased now. The store had three names over the years. It was first known as Gower's at the Bridge. After Tom went into business with his dad it was known as W. H. Gower and Son. At Waldo's death in 1964 it became Gower's Inc. Most of us from Grifton will always call it Gower's Store. As we wish that time did not move so quickly. Nor take so much.

Chapter Nine

GOWER'S BRIDGE

It was once a bustling area in that place where the Contentnea Creek divides Pitt County from Lenoir. The bridge ushered you into Grifton. Steam boats still traveled the creek when that bridge was built. They traveled as far as Snow Hill bringing freight and produce. The bridge had to open to let the bigger boats pass through so it was designed with an overhead counter weight to help raise it. The weight was mechanically lowered and caused that section of the highway to rise and allow for clearance and safe passage.

The real name is Cameron Bridge but most know it as Gower's because of the store located next to it and described in the earlier chapter of this book. Let's take a closer look at that business. W.H. Gower, or Waldo, operated the store on the left and just across the creek leading from town. It was much smaller than present day grocery stores but as stated before it did offer everything one needed. Two gas pumps were aligned in front of the business. There was even a wired cage on the premise where Waldo kept his pet monkey. The animal wore a collar to attach a lease and he and his master were quite the town fixtures as they visited often. No one could control that monkey but Waldo himself. The monkey was very mischievous indeed and once bit my finger while I tried to feed him a peanut.

He did build that oyster bar out over the creek and parallel to the highway bridge. It was about fifty feet long. You can still find some shells there by the banks even now if you look closely. It was there that he kept the cabin boat tied up near the bridge that bore his name. Many of his friends were treated to a ride on the creek. That vessel was a large one and it's hard to imagine a boat that size coming down that water today. I don't know how he did it.

The stories of that bridge are deeply woven and an integral part of the town of Grifton. I recall a few myself. On March 18, 1957, and under the cover of the darkness of night, it appeared that a person had hung their self from the upper structure of that bridge and the body was dangling over the highway. Many calls went in to the Grifton police station reporting the tragedy. Some recall that Lynn Gower, who was Tom's wife, was the first to report it. It was a horrifying sight to witness. Herb Adams was the police chief at the time and he summoned a State highway patrolman by the name of Tayloe who lived in Grifton to get the body down.

It turned out that the body was a well placed dummy. Someone had hung an effigy on Gower's Bridge. Upon further and careful investigation a laundry mark was found on the clothing. The identifying mark was labeled GCS7 and was from Pressley Laundry. That label belonged to my dad. George Cisroe Sugg was the father of Tommy,

Margaret, Dot, and myself. Our father was too old to climb and never considered a suspect. But my brother was known for his pranks and was questioned heavily by the police. He offered that perhaps his dad had discarded the pants and someone else had retrieved them from the dump. The Barwick boys from the Lenoir side of the creek also remain suspect but they refuse to talk about it to this day. The case remains in the cold files.

When the town Shad Festival came into being the bridge became a trademark of sorts. The festival logo of "Eat Mo Shad" appeared in bright paint up on the bridge transom. No one admits to that graffiti either. There is a new bridge that crosses the creek now. It does not raise but just brings travel into the town. But the stories are there and remain for the telling.

Chapter Ten

COWARD BRIDGE

You would hardly know it was there. It would take searching in the right place to see any remaining evidence of its once existence. Coward Bridge. There have been other bridges that spanned the Contentnea Creek over the years and Coward was certainly an important part of the history for our small town. It was not yet named Grifton in those days. It was known as Bell's Ferry. The bridge was not built without fight. Fight was also what destroyed it.

The Contentnea divides the counties of Pitt and Lenoir. Old maps show a much different topography and route of travel many years ago than now. A dirt road took you from our side of the creek to the highway that led north to Greenville. The road paralleled it and never lost sight of the water. It passed a seine beach that I can still remember. It was about three hundred yards long and white with sand. It was a very pretty place. You could see Yellow Banks just across on the Lenoir side. I was a boy scout and J.Q. Patrick was my leader. One winter day in January he decided to take our troop to the seine beach on the Contentnea to pass a swimming test. We hurriedly passed our test that very cold day and ran for the huge bon fire he had built on the banks. Never has a fire felt so good. A portion of that old road is still there and used today. It was paved several years back.

Seining operations were once quite common and especially during shad season. A gentle slope from land down to the water was necessary. It allowed for the pulling of the seine. There was usually a ferry close by and common for the time. I recall the one at Street's Ferry. It was powered by an automobile engine and carried only one car across the creek each way. It was a daring ride floating across the eerie and dark water. The creek was once such a crucial part of existence.

It was the year 1849 and a bridge was deemed beneficial for our area. It would open much quicker access to the nearby and larger towns of New Bern and Greenville for the south side. It would also allow better passage to points south for those on our side of the creek. Court records show that a petition was made by the commissioners of both counties to construct one. In those days the only way across the creek was by way of a ferry. It was operated by a man named Warren Bell. The ferry ran its operation just above Yellow Banks near Tick Bite. Chosen for the sight of the proposed bridge. Mr. Bell vehemently opposed it. He knew it would stop the need of his ferry there and necessitate the relocation of it. He took the commissioners to court in opposition. The fight for the bridge had begun.

Coward's Landing was about a mile downstream and on the south and Lenoir side of the creek. The Cowards were large land owners in the area and much of their property bordered the Contentnea. The bridge would be built there and named in their honor. The court eventually did rule in favor of the petition to build. Warren Bell had lost his fight and forced to move closer to where the current bridge now spans the creek. The community was then referred to as Bell's Ferry. Construction began with a total price not to exceed six hundred dollars. That bridge opened the way to places like Pitchkettle, Streets Ferry, Cowpen, and Vanceboro. It was a key beginning to better travel.

The Civil war loomed on the horizon and Grifton did not escape it. There are stories of a large encampment near our town. They sacrificed the bridge and destroyed it to slow the pace of the Yankee soldiers. That vital passageway was gone. I am kin to the Coward family and my cousin, Allen Barwick, told me that he had once seen the old timber pilings of the bridge back in the 50's when the water was low. He had been fishing and it was visible protruding from the water. It is said that some of the iron breastwork is still there. There is a bit of clearing where it touched the land. The area is full of Cyprus which do grow very slow. It is the location of the bridge. Almost forgotten. Except for the penning of the recollections and its telling of history again.

Chapter Eleven

THE CHURCH BELL

The sound of the pealing bell would soon be heard in our little town. A prominent citizen by the name of Moses Spivey enlisted the help of Albert Coward and together they built the Grifton Methodist Church. It was constructed with all locally grown and sawed wood including the shingles. A separate belfry was built into the design and waited for the bell to arrive. The location of this church is the existing main building of the town museum which is next to the creek.

Grifton was called Bells Ferry in the early years and did not change until just three years before the church was completed. The name was derived from a man who operated the ferry just across from town on the other side of the Contentnea. It was located near the site of the present day boat landing. That area was the center of much activity in that period of our history. A large dock was situated there which accommodated all the freight that the steamboats hauled up and down the water from New Bern to Snow Hill.

Main Street ran parallel to the creek and was the site of many homes of that day. Dr. W.W. Dawson advised moving away from that close location of the water to promote better health. The town was now called Grifton and a rail road had recently established a route through and it took most of the business away from the steam boats. The bell would come by steam and rail. There was no other means of transporting such a heavy item at the time.

Moses was just thirty five years old when he built the church and he purchased and donated the bell to the congregation. It was an exciting day when it arrived. It had been ordered from the C.S. Bell company in Hillsboro, Ohio. That place is known for bell making and even celebrate their heritage with a Festival of the Bells each year around the fourth of July. This particular company is still in business today. They employed just two people when the Grifton bell was made and had a total payroll of $7.00 per week.

The bell was built in the late 1800's, is a number 40, and weighs approximately 1300 pounds. While most are made of bronze, Mr. Bell developed an iron alloy that attracted customers from all over the world. The cost of the alloy was much cheaper than the bronze, lasted longer, and had a more desirable tone. It was still a big and heavy item and belfry towers were often cause for concern. Since they were most likely built of wood they became unstable over time. The Methodist began to fear for their own tower after a while. This was about the time the town began to move away from the creek and to higher ground and that included the church. They would build a new building and had to make a decision about the bell.

The Barwick family were pillars in the Methodist church and it was decided they would house the bell until the church could once again find a place for it. It was loaded on an ox cart and passed across the Contentnea by way of the old bridge near the boat landing and finally made its way to the Barwick farm. It was put to good use there. Every day its toll would signal the time to begin work. It also rang promptly at twelve noon for lunch and again at one to return to the fields. It also rang to announce special occasions. If the wind was just right the sound of the chiming of the bell could be heard quite plainly into Grifton. Miss May Coward Barwick was the grandmother of the Barwick boys and she was the chief and very punctual ringer. Townsfolk set their watches by the ringing bell.

The Methodist Church is one of the oldest churches in town. The congregation built its third building during the 1950s. Bill DesVerges managed a planing mill in the Tick Bite area near town and was instrumental in bringing the bell back home where it was remounted in the new belfry. There it served the purpose of calling the church members to worship. That dangling rope was always a source of temptation to us town youngsters.

The congregation outgrew that sanctuary and the building was to be torn down to make way for a new one at that same location. Cox Trailers was located close by and agreed to store the bell until a new place was made ready. The bell was loved and its existence never forgotten. The new church was built and the bell was once again brought home where it belonged. It remains there to this day and is housed atop a brick pillar and close to the ground. The museum in town houses a painting of the original Methodist church. It is done by artist, Bob Pittman, and copied from a photograph that belonged to his father who was also a member of the original church. I feel so fortunate to have this knowledge of the bell and church. My sister, Dorothy Reeves, wrote the history of the Methodist church and Allen Barwick kept fastidious records. The Barwicks and Bob Pittman are my cousins.

The old church bell has served such purpose over all these years. There were no early sirens and this bell became the sound of the town. It is mostly silent now. Guarded to extend its life. When I return to Grifton I always ride by the church and look to see the bell in its place on the grounds. The last time it rang was in December of 2012. It rang twenty six times. One for each of the victims of the Sandy Hook shooting. The town was hushed at the sound. The bell still commands attention.

Chapter Twelve

THE LOG CABIN

The path is still there. Coming from Grifton and just past Gaskin's Landing it leads off to the right. The building is no longer standing but I can almost see it in my mind's eye. It was a log cabin built not far from where the Contentnea Creek and Neuse River meet. It was in the very early 1900's when a group of Grifton business men, the likes of Dr. W.W. Dawson, Tom Gardner, J. R Harvey, and other of the town business owners felt the need for a meeting place. These men worked hard for six days a week and desired a place to relax and play cards. They wanted to fish, hunt and cook what they bagged. A forerunner of the modern day need for a man cave.

The best that I can recall it was about forty feet long and maybe thirty feet wide. The south end had a huge brick fireplace used for heat and cooking. Iron pots were hung over the open fire for stews and such. The cabin was made from logs harvested in that very area. The roof was made of tin and windows allowed for light but there was no electricity and lanterns were used at night. The woods surrounding that cabin were full of large oak trees and the grounds were quite beautiful. There were other trees too, almost any indigenous to the area. Cyprus, water oak, white oak, hickory, pine, gum ash, and pecan. Wild blueberries grew nearby and other food that attracted plenty of game. Turkey, wood ducks and squirrels. Deer had not yet populated the area in those days. It was a fine place to hunt.

The path to the cabin led around and past it for about a quarter of a mile and to a lake that was full of fish. The lake was a deep part of the slough that flowed from the Contentnea during high water. It was known as Silver Lake. The water was about two hundred yards long and perhaps twenty feet wide. There was always water in it no matter how dry it was. The lake remains today. I have often parked my vehicle there to hunt and it proved to be great hunting ground. In times of drought you can walk all around it and walking south will take you to the Neuse. You will cross several ridges and sloughs and they run parallel to the river. That always helped me with navigation.

The cabin was used by many people and different purposes over the course of the time that it stood. It was almost like a community building and used as those in Grifton saw fit. It was treated well and kept clean for the most part. During the 1930's my own boy scout troop used it for camping out. We swam in the Contentnea Creek's seine beach and passed our swimming test there. Our scout master was J. Q. Patrick, brother to Henry Oglesby's wife. He was devoted and spent a lot of time with us. The troop had some good pillow fights in that cabin.

One of the most memorable events in that old place was a party so big that many out of town folks came. Since they had no idea how to get to the building in the woods we had to place precise direction markers to guide them. An old wind up Victrola provided the music for this event. This was back in the 1940's and it proved to be a fine night and is still vivid in my memory.

That cabin cost about three hundred dollars to construct in those days but to reflect back to it is priceless. It meant so much to so many in Grifton. I doubt if any of us know who really owned the place but the foresight to build it is appreciated by a lot of folks. Many now still living recall it. There is a drawing of the old log cabin done by Van Tucker and it is on display in Mike Gaskin's office which is located just down the road from where the place stood.

That creek road is still dirt and the area is full of rich Grifton history. The cabin in the woods is a wonderful part of that history and the story of it is worth the telling here once more. To remember it and the men who gave it to us.

Chapter Thirteen

TYPHOON COBRA

Grifton has always sacrificed some of her own for American wars. Many of my generation served in World War II. Waldo Gower was the son of W. H. Gower who ran the store on the Lenoir County side of Contentnea Creek. He was called Bud and we grew up together. He lived just three houses down on the opposite side of the street from me. We served at the same time but on different ships. Our plans were to meet up as soon as we could. It was in December of 1944 and America was in deep conflict with the Japanese.

We were both part of Admiral William Halsey's third fleet task force 38. Bull Halsey led the greatest fleet there ever was. A task force is a group of ships. Destroyers, cruisers, aircraft carriers, and battleships. Our task force had just dealt a damaging blow to the Japanese. Our location was in the South Pacific and near the Philippines. Halsey received word that a typhoon was headed our way. We call them hurricanes on the east coast. The powerful and deadly storms are called typhoons in that area of the

Pacific. Admiral Halsey had received conflicting tracks of the storm. He listened to the wrong information and decided to hide our task force in the middle of Typhoon Cobra. There were seventy five war ships that would try and ride out the powerful storm in formation. It proved to be a deadly mistake.

I was stationed on the USS battleship North Carolina. The battleships of the force are there to protect the air craft carriers and to bombard enemy positions with their nine sixteen inch guns that are mounted in three turrets. These ships are plenty sea worthy and carry enough fuel to keep the smaller ships going such as the destroyers which has the function of antisubmarine defense. When sonar detects submarine signals they immediately drop depth chargers. Their small size limits them to only enough fuel for six or seven days. They depend on the larger ships for refueling.

I saw this transfer take place many times. The vessel would come alongside the larger one and only separated by a few yards. A line is passed over to secure and then the fuel hose is pulled and connected from the supply ship. The seas must be relatively calm or the process can be in vain. I have seen hoses break and black crude oil spray the hull of the receive ship. It is tough to do in rough seas and proved impossible during Typhoon Cobra.

It was December 18 and the refueling operation had begun. A ship needs to be at more than half full to weigh herself down in stormy seas. Some of the ships were at very low gauge. The recent attack had depleted fuel supply. The typhoon was bearing down quicker than any of us had imagined. The Sunday skies of the 17th were dark and brooding. The choppy seas were now forceful. The wind had picked up speed so furiously the ships began to toss violently. The hoses snapped in two. Refueling efforts were in vain and had to be ceased. The ships low on fuel would ride high in the waves and were at their own mercy.

Typhoon Cobra was bearing down on task force 38 just as Halsey had planned. It was now the 18th and we were indeed hidden from the Japanese. Visibility was so poor that you could only see yards away. The rains were torrential and so pelting it would cut your face. It blew sideways in the winds that reached brutal speeds of well over one hundred miles per hour. The waves were merciless and would pick us up with each rise and slam us back vehemently back into the sea. The usual routine of the ship had dissipated. The mess hall was shut down because the ship pitched so badly. The cooks made sandwiches and delivered them at certain points throughout the ship.

I was an electrician on board and had access to almost any place as long as my tool box was visible. I made my way up to the conning tower which is about seventy five feet above the water line. It was a good vantage point to see the full fury of Cobra. From there I could look up and see the waves crest above me and higher still. I watched as they crashed down viciously onto the deck of the ship and the entire thing would disappear under a sea of ferocious water. Any life on that deck would have been quickly swept away. At times I had seen enemy planes fly over close enough to see the pilot goggles and was not afraid. That night of Typhoon Cobra I feared for my life. I cannot imagine what the sailors of the smaller ships endured. We had lost sight of the others in the raging storm. We knew some ships were lost. We learned of this through the PA.

The storm finally calmed. It had formed on December 14 and subsided on the 19th. It was at long last over and the USS North Carolina had come through with only minor damage. Others were not so lucky. Three of our destroyers were lost. USS Monaghan. USS Spence. The USS Hull. One hundred forty six planes were either lost overboard or damaged beyond repair. Worse yet, seven hundred and ninety lives were lost. Eighty sailors were injured. The mighty third fleet was crippled. Cobra is also remembered as Halsey's typhoon and was the worst enemy he faced. He was subjected to a court of inquiry aboard ship. He was found guilty of committing an error of judgment in sailing us into the heart of a typhoon. His action was declared as stress of war. They stopped short of any further sanctions.

The USS North Carolina was eventually rescued and survives as a museum. She stands proudly in a cove of water in Wilmington. A grass roots effort brought her home to her namesake state. The children at Grifton School gave dimes to preserve her. The war was indeed a time of growing up for those of us who served. I am grateful to have come home to our little town at the end of it all. Some did not fare as well in that awful storm. Waldo Gower did not come home again. Bud was on the USS Hull when it went down. My friend was gone.

Chapter Fourteen

GRIFTON V.F.W.

Our little town has always supplied men and women who fought for our country. A lot of us began to return home after World War II. I had served in the South Pacific on a battleship called the USS North Carolina. It had been a horrific time for many. Some saw the need for aid and a local chapter of the Veterans of Foreign War was established to help in meeting some of those needs. The Casey brothers of our town, Ed and Don, were instrumental in organizing that first unit. VFW posts are located across the country and serve as a place where veterans can meet, tend to business, socialize, and have recreation. It is a valuable addition for the vets of a community and it was time for one in our area.

A small tin building located near Mill Branch Bridge was used for that first headquarters. It was a very modest building with dirt floors and was used for quite a while. The opportunity finally came for a better structure. John Waters had purchased a 24 X 30 building from the DuPont plant in nearby Lenoir County. They had used it for a canteen. Many will remember that it was located next to Buddy's

Barbecue. It was a much desired improvement and in 1953 the members added space for a kitchen and bathrooms on the back of it.

There was a lot of pride in the place and many of us veterans found pleasure in being there. Booths were installed on one side of the main room so that patrons could sit and eat. A juke box was purchased and played the great songs of the 50's. You could make the selection of your choice and it did not cost a dime. Every month, on a Saturday night, the members would meet there to eat and dance. It was usually a group of twenty to twenty five people to gather. The building was perfect for that size group.

The food was always good. Tucker McGlohorn, and Walter and Wilbur Murphy, were usually the cooks. Five dollars would buy a meal for two people that included rib eye steaks, baked potato, and iced tea. It was a good deal when you added the free music and a space to dance while surrounded by friends. The group usually cleared away the dishes and the music began. The popular dances of the early days were the bop, the slop, and the twist. Line dancing also became in style there.

Chuck Sherron was a dance instructor that lived in Grifton and he taught most of us the dance steps. It was customary for everyone there to hit the dance floor as soon as the jukebox cranked out a tune. I especially loved watching the participation of the twist. The group would form a circle while one would get in the center and perform their unique version. We also enjoyed the limbo. We had made our own stick which would be raised high and then lowered after each dancer had a turn. It was a lot of fun and was a sure way to bring on the laughter. I am pleased to remember that I was very good at it, but have to admit that it was Geri Casey that usually won.

I am happy to know that we had a VFW chapter. It was very satisfying and brought together a group that had seen some difficult times and understood each other. War seemed far away when we gathered in that small place. It is still meeting these days and in the same building. The small town of Ayden is close by and they have joined with our chapter. They still cook meals from that kitchen. A ladies auxiliary has also formed and add to the importance of the group. Our particular chapter is known as the Gower, Sumrell, Wiley Post. It honors those who lost their lives in WWII. Grifton still supplies those who defend our country. I do not take that lightly and never will. It makes me proud. I am very proud.

Chapter Fifteen

BUILDING A DREAM

One would hardly know it was there. The paved street leading to it ends abruptly. A mass of uninviting briers, small trees and shrubs grown in the pathway to prevent further access. A utilitarian farm gate is permanently closed across the entrance. No one is welcome there any longer. It is like a tomb now. It was not this way once. On the other side of that closed gate lay what was once a dream. The minds and hands and feet of the citizens of our town took it from a wish and to reality. Grifton had her own golf course.

Fishing was the popular recreation of our town. That changed when Cecil Lilley and Bill Daw moved to Grifton. Bill was the manager of the bank in town. Cecil worked for the nearby DuPont plant. They were from towns that had courses and both loved the game. Cecil had moved from nearby Farmville and had caddied for his dad at an early age. Sam Jr. McLawhorn was the only other golfer I knew. He was a professional ball player and had traveled extensively and played the game. They would get together and imagine how nice it would be to have a course in our town. It moved from fantasy to a plan as they talked to other locals and promoted interest. A fevered pitch ensued and plans were made.

There was absolutely no money to build a golf course. It was a shoe string budget at its best. The grass roots efforts began to sell stock to make enough money for a down payment on land. A site had been picked out just north of town. It belonged to the Gower family. They were willing to sell in hopes it would increase value of their remaining land. Sam Nelson owned property nearby and he contributed heavily and for the same reason. Construction started around 1956. It was an exciting time.

It was to be a nine hole course. There was definitely not money for more. A board of directors was appointed. We borrowed heavily on this project but had good faith in what we were doing and lots of high hopes. We had no plan for a design layout. Relying totally on the expertise of those established golfers. Cecil, Bill, and Sam, Jr. planned it. The DuPont plant had engineers and other tradesmen who became valuable in the process. They worked diligently. All of it was volunteer labor. Grifton citizens put in untold hours of hard, sweaty, and back breaking labor. The women of the community worked right along with us men. My wife, Edna, helped sprig the grass along with so many others. The vision had really caught and we worked undeterred. We were consumed with our effort and determined to make it happen. The cost was a fraction of what it would have been without such committed workers that willingly gave their time. It was unity at its best.

The course was finally ready to play in 1960. It was an

exciting time and we held our first championship. It was expected that Cecil would win and he did not disappoint. Others watched him and over time learned to play the game. It proved to be good fun. I had never played before. This is the course I caught a love for golf and spent many days on those greens. Membership continued to grow as it caught on. We had every right to be proud of our accomplishment there on the rise of that land. The dream had come true. Grifton finally had a golf course.

Club memberships were sold to help finance the day to day operation. Volunteer labor continued to keep us going. Ed Reeves was the greens chairman. He was to keep them in good shape for playing and he took his role very serious. A pro shop was built and sold soft drinks and snacks, It carried a small line of necessary golfing equipment. Our golf carts were the pull behind kind. We certainly could not afford a pro but eventually did hire an elderly man by the name of Ned McLawhorn to run the store. He must have been eighty years old but worked every day that he could. Members would fill in on days that came that he could not be there. We were eventually able to obtain a license to sell beer. State law prohibited the sale of it on Sundays before noon. One Sunday I filled in for Ned and I was unaware of the rule. Two agents walked in and I served them a couple of beers. We were reported and almost lost our license. It took a lot of explaining.

We were eventually able to hire a pro to run the place and began charging green fees to aid in the finances. We were doing well financially. Nice houses were built in the section surrounding the course. The country club area became a desirable location to live. Board members changed and progressive ideas were always on the table. Players began to want eighteen holes to play. Additional land was purchased to make it happen. Interest rates in those days was a soaring six per cent. We did not get a fixed rate. Our rate was six plus prime and it soared. The prime went to seventeen per cent. We had aggressively invested in the additional nine, a swimming pool, and a tennis court. We had to face reality. We were overwhelmed and could not afford the money we owed. The Grifton Golf Course could not meet its obligations. We were devastated.

The bank held the mortgage. It was eventually sold to Wiley and Mike Gaskins at that time. It was a good arrangement. They were local and had the heavy duty equipment to finish the back nine holes. They changed the name to Indian Trails. Paying homage to Grifton's early history of the Tuscarora Indians. It was thriving when they finally sold it to Brad Brooks and Eddie Wheeler. It closed in 2014. I do not know why.

It is all grown over now. Deeply buried. The old dream is entombed in brambles. Trees have reclaimed the labor of our hands. The greens would be long gone. I wonder the condition of the clubhouse or if it even still stands. The pool and tennis courts would be wasted away. Along with the pride that was. A gate stands guard to the decay on that hill. To keep out those who no longer belong. We are not welcome there any longer. Until a new dreamer comes along. Perhaps to uncover and restore the glory of the Indian Trails. I hope they do. I wish they would.

Chapter Sixteen

GASKINS LANDING

It is one of the four historical sites on the Jolly Ole Field Road. There is Jolly Ole Field itself, Ed Rutledge's shack site, and that of the old log cabin. You reach Gaskins Landing by turning off highway 118 and drive below the Mike Gaskins farm. You travel left where the road forks and the entrance is on the right and guarded by a metal gate. The path on the other side leads to the Contentnea Creek. Most fishing folk from the area know the spot well.

Mike has done much work to accommodate the area anglers and even those who love to picnic by the water. He made space for a nice parking lot, placed picnic tables, benches, and trash cans. Most come for the water though and he built boat ramps for easy access. He sells membership fees for a reasonable price and to help regulate the place.

The landing is located at an area of the creek known as the Narrows because the water is indeed not broad there at all and with many twists and turns. It is also lined on both sides with huge trees whose branches are so lofty that they almost touch overhead. There are many Cyprus trees there that are old enough they could have stood watch when the Tuscarora Indians once walked these banks. It must have been a treacherous place for the old steam freight boats that used these waters all those years ago. The area was a drop off site for cargo.

Because it is so narrow the water flow is quite rapid and deep in sections and during the heat of summer the water is much cooler there. It is a known fact that cool water holds oxygen better and for that reason fish swim to that particular area. It is a region for largemouth bass, river robins, and some striped bass. It has been a popular fishing spot over the years. One of the best fishing holes is where the Contentea Creek flows into the Neuse River and this landing has the nearest place to launch a boat to reach these waters.

Grifton is the site of the Shad Festival each spring and hickory shad go upstream to spawn. Fisherman take to the waters from February through April trying to catch the winning shad for the festival prize of hooking the heaviest one. Quite often the winning entry is from the Narrows. It is also a place for fun and a practical joke or two. I have been made aware of one that I can share.

The gate to the landing is battery operated and complete with a solar panel to charge the battery. You enter by use of a remote key much like the ones for a car. You have enough time to enter and then it closes behind you. It is told that area resident and frequent user of the place, Bobby Bowen, took a friend to the area to fish one day and when they pulled up to the gate he told his friend that the gate would open by saying the words, "Shad at Gaskins." With a straight face, and the remote hidden in his pocket, he demonstrated. The gate opened beautifully. He then challenged his companion to give it a try and he did so. The gate did not open. Bobby told him that he was not saying the words right and he coached him on the proper tone. The friend followed and to his delight the gate magically opened but he was unaware of the hidden remote Bobby had secretly pushed in his pocket.

The friend later wanted to impress his own friends at his new found knowledge of gaining entrance to the popular fishing place. He pulls up unto the entrance, rolls down his truck window and in his practiced voice says to the gate, "Shad at Gaskins." The gate never opened even after several tries. He later relayed his failure to Bobby who just shook his head and told him he just wasn't saying it right. It took a while but the friend became red faced when he realized he had been the subject of a Bowen prank. I will not reveal the name of the innocent party in this story but most would know the poor fellow.

The landing is indeed another part of the rich Grifton history that is found on Jolly Ole Field Road. It is a lucky soul that has experienced them all. I am such a fellow.

Chapter Seventeen

THE POLITICALLY DEAD

Our little town always took her politics seriously. To the point that we buried the losers. I suppose you could call that dead serious. It was all in good clean fun. To everyone except perhaps the losers. The election of mayor and town board members could become quite heated. Campaign could render friend against friend. Election day would come and the winner declared. It would be at the close of that day when the mischievousness took place under the cover of darkness.

Something mysterious would take place the day after a victorious vote for the winner. New graves would mysteriously appear and prominently displayed on Queen Street. Freshly mounded graves. For all to see as they passed by. The citizens of the town looked forward to the viewing on the day after the vote. Grifton had one person who could write humorous epitaphs and that one was enlisted after each election. To humorously toast the losing candidates. We probably should not have done it. It should not have been such fun. It really was though.

One year was an especially heated campaign. Wiley Gaskins had been mayor for quite some time and chose not to run again. He thought it fair to give someone else an opportunity to govern our little town. George Saleeby and Ed Haseley had decided to throw their hat into the political ring vying for that seat. Julius Chauncey decided to enter Wiley as a write in candidate two weeks before the election. He promoted the good that he had been for the town. It became a hotly contested race between some of Grifton's finest.

Election day came and the vote was cast. Wiley became mayor for another term. It was a bit of a bruising loss. It stung a little more on the day after. Overnight the dirt was secretly brought in and the graves appeared. They were located mid Queen Street near Murphy Brothers. Some elections had two candidates buried in the same grave. Not on this year. Saleeby had his own mock grave. The epitaph read,

> Saleeby has been running for mayor
> Ever since he came to town.
> This time he thought the poll was right
> And he put his money down.
> But when the votes were counted
> the strangest thing ever heard.
> Only two men were running
> And George came in third.

I had forgotten the words of the makeshift fake and cardboard tombstone long ago. Some folks remembered it well and told me. Mike Gaskins said his dad, Wiley, was one of the mock political morticians. It was not the dignity displayed in the day of George Washington or Abraham Lincoln. Nor was it the cutthroat that politics has become today. It also did not cause wars. It was just good clean fun between friends.

Chapter Eighteen

JOHN LAWSON LEGACY DAYS

Some people have lived in Grifton all their lives and have never touched the waters of the Contentnea Creek. They remain unaware of the rich past of that historic winding body that helped put Grifton on the map. The celebration of the John Lawson Legacy Days is determined to change that. He was an English explorer who was captured by the Tuscarora Indians and executed in or very near the town of Grifton. There are those who wished to remember him and the John Lawson Legacy Days were born. It is an annual event and the two days continue to grow in popularity each year. Residents, Tim and Mary Grace Bright, have helped organize a tour and are aided by several volunteers to keep the valuable chronicles of our past alive and remembered.

Tours by boat are available on Saturday if the water proves deep enough to navigate. It is a ride of abundant recall of times once lived in our area. Some of the sites on the tour were here when our town was called Bell's Ferry. That name derived from Warren Bell who operated a ferry across the creek. The adventure begins at the boat landing once you have been seated onto a boat. The journey takes you upstream and to the sites that wait like ghosts wanting to tell their story one more time.

Look directly across from the landing and there is the place called The Bottom. It includes a fairly new campground, an old cemetery, and once upon a time the area was the home of a saloon of sorts called The Green Door. James Braxton operated the small building with a literal green painted door and the main business of this establishment was to sell whisky by the drink. Grifton Bridge, also known as Sawmill Bridge, spanned the creek at this point and connected Pitt to Lenoir County. The May Bell had a docking place on the creek where the old saw mill was.

Alf Coward was born in the Bottom and he is buried there also. He was well remembered by many of the town. That bridge is long gone but some of the footings still remain. At the foot of the bridge on the Lenoir side was a store operated by Albert G. Coward. My family and the Barwick boys are descendents of his. My mother once told me that Albert had two or three children before he was old enough to vote. Just to the north of the bridge was that sawmill and a freight boat by the name of May Bell which was built and often docked there. It carried cargo from New Bern to Snow Hill on a regular route. A replica of this boat is now housed in the Grifton museum.

Next on the tour is the Atlantic Coast Line railroad trestle. It could be mechanically opened to allow steam freight boats a safe passage. That trestle has a history dating back over one hundred years. On the south side there was a wooden water tank to supply train boilers. Gower's Bridge comes into view as we continue our excursion upstream and the site of the former Gower's store is on the south side of it. The proper name for the bridge is really Cameron Bridge but most Grifton people call it Gower's. The old bridge was torn down many years ago but the many stories it left behind still remain.

About a half mile further up is a large slough on the left and it is called Tucker's Cove. It was named after Mr. Tom Tucker who was the father of Dr. Tucker, Ben, Glendel, and one daughter. Patrick's Landing is located about another half mile up and on the right. It bears the name after Allen Patrick. The family loved fishing and kept their boats tied to an old cypress tree there. The marks where the iron mooring rings were located are still visible to this day. The names are considered important because the lives of these people were so entwined with this town by the creek.

About fifty yards up on the Pitt County side is a place where a bank seems to rise straight up from the water for about twenty five feet and the water drops to a dramatic twelve feet just inches from the bank itself. That bank is a very dark blue and it is believed that passing boat captain's gave it the identifying name of Blue Banks. Another cove lies just fifty yards away and is called McCotter's Cove. The land around it belongs to Grifton resident, Bette McCotter. The upstream tour ends at the newer bridge across Highway 11 which now bypasses traffic around and away from our town.

Space does not permit an expedition of the water downstream of the landing. I wish it did. That history is just as rich. From there is a bridge called Mill Branch and it passes over a stream that once housed a grist mill. Just below the bridge was a road that followed the creek all the way to the Coward bridge site. It used to cross the creek just before reaching Tick Bite. It was burned during the Civil War to prevent the Union army from crossing. Old records state that when planning to build this bridge a budget of six hundred dollars was agreed by the Pitt and Lenoir Counties. One can only imagine the cost of that today. Travelers from New Bern used this bridge when riding to Greenville by the road that followed alongside the creek and passed through our bustling little town. The community of Tick Bite is on the Lenoir side and the seine beach is on the Pitt. That beach used to have seining operation and pretty white sand which made it a popular place to swim.

These are some of the sites of the heritage of the Contentnea that beg for their place in history to be heard. The scenery is perhaps best viewed from a boat. The October opportunity of John Lawson Legacy Days are a good time to climb aboard and hear their stories and see them come alive again. A chance to experience our past one more time.

People
of
Grifton

A place without people is
just a ghost town.
Not much to write about.
There were so many stories of
Grifton citizens I could share.
More than space would allow.
It was the people of Grifton who
dreamed and shaped her.
Gave the town her heart beat.
Made the heart skip a beat
in some instances.
We all had a story.
I have chosen a few to share.

Chapter Nineteen

EDWIN REEVES

He was one of the best friends I ever had. Also the most gullible. He was my brother in law which made him an easy target for my love and aggravation of playing pranks. I call it my dark side. Ed came to Grifton from down at Ivanhoe and married my sister, Dorothy. He worked for the local DuPont plant and loved fishing as much as I did. We spent a lot of time casting for largemouth bass in the Contentnea Creek. He taught me the art of jigger fishing. We even stocked the ponds at the golf course with bass. I thought the world of him and did love yanking his chain. He was so easy and almost came to expect it. I choose to write about two of my favorites.

This happened in the early years of knee replacements. Most folks thought long and hard about it in those days. It was no easy procedure. Ed Reeves trusted quickly and could be easy to fleece on a telephone. This was in the day before cell phones and caller ID. He also had a bad knee and was considering surgery. His concern spilled over into talking to everyone he met about it. Eventually everybody in the county knew he had a poor knee it seemed. The call that came following did not seem to surprise him.

Mr. Reeves, I disguised my voice and tried to sound quite professional when I called. I told him that I understood surgery was pending. Went on to tell Ed that I represented a company in Australia and they had an injection that was an alternate to surgery and worked as well. My brother in law listened with interest and asked about it. He was told by my voice on the phone that a serum taken from the knee joints of a kangaroo would solve his problem. Two injections would be all it took. I reassured him there would be no pain or danger. Ed did ask for a name of someone who had tried it. That caught me by surprise and I saw a name on the television screen just then. Art Linkletter, I replied. That certainly satisfied him. I told him he could ask his surgeon for the details of the injection. Ed immediately made an appointment. He walked into the office with great confidence armed with this wealth of information about the kangaroo serum. The doctor righted that untruth immediately. It was not until after the knee replacement that I told him what I had done. He was such a good natured sport that he was not too mad.

It should have been enough. I got him one more time though. His daughter, Olivia, had an afghan hound named Josh. Bred for sight hunting. That breed is not common in our area. She moved down to the outer banks and could not take the dog with her. He stayed with Ed and lived to be quite up there in age. Josh was about fifteen years old when the getting got really good for playing another hoax. It had been a while.

Josh had gotten very feeble. He could barely stand on his own and Ed had to help him. He even spoon fed him while he lay in the chair they shared. My brother in law was foolish over that dog. I enlisted my sister in law, Jean, to help me with this one. She is an office manager for several lawyers and she has learned to be convincing. She called Ed one night after dinner. Told him she understood that he had an afghan hound. The vet had told her so. The only registered male around. Jean went on to tell him that she wanted to breed her female. He could have the pick of the resulting litter. Ed Reeves was speechless.

He was somewhat stunned and told her that his dog was too old for such pleasure. I just had to feed him his supper with a spoon, he informed her. He can't even stand up. I don't think he can do what you're asking. Jean has learned not to take no for an answer. He finally relented and told her that she could bring her female but not to expect any miracles. He hung up the phone and told Dorothy that Josh needed a bath in the tub. That the old boy had a date. He shook his head, wondering what he had done. He had swallowed that one hook, line, and sinker. Dot was in on the prank and burst out laughing. Me and my wife, Edna, were also sitting there at his house when that call came. It was just as we had planned and we came unglued. That mating gig was up.

Edwin Reeves was one good man. He never did get upset with the practical jokes we played on him. Laughed with us instead. Life was made better with his presence in it. He is gone too. Like so many of the others in our town. He was a light that still burns. I see it clearly from where I tell of him.

Chapter Twenty

BILL TUCKER

What do they call a duck in Virginia? He would ask that question to everyone that he met. A duck. That was his straightforward answer. Bill Tucker is fondly remembered for setting up all those he knew with that particular joke. He told it over and over. You knew it was coming when you saw him. He was born to Ben and Ruth on April 5, 1939. They were indeed his parents but he also belonged to the town. He was as much a fixture in Grifton as any of the buildings or landmarks. He always put a smile on the faces of those he met and he met most all that came here.

The Tucker family lived up on the hill past the yellow Catholic church and on the left just before the road curves to the right. They also had a daughter, Earle Tucker Hines, who now resides in Greenville. Bill kept to his daily routine of walking down and through the town in the mornings right after his breakfast. Rarely did you see him riding in a car because he preferred the pace of his own walk. He did not drive. Grifton was a thriving place during Bill's lifetime and there were a lot more stores than there are now.

The first stop was his dad's business located on the corner of Queen and Highland. It was a sizable gas station with a Pure Oil sign hanging out front near the pumps. They had a garage and repair shop in the rear and sold automotives and other related items. It was called Tucker Brothers because Ben and his brother, Glendel, owned it together. Bill would usually spend most of the morning there and loved to talk to all the patrons.

One day Bill was in the front of the store while the brothers were busy helping customers in the back. A hat salesman came through the door with a large case of caps. He spotted Bill, cleared his throat, and asked if he was Mr. Tucker? Bill innocently replied that he was. The salesman was hoping to sell a few cases of the caps and he asked if he could show Mr. Tucker his array. In his nasal and unique voice he said yes. The man unpacked about thirty of the hats and showed them to a very interested Bill Tucker. He was quite dramatic in his presentation on the merits of his wares. He finally finished and proudly asked this particular Mr. Tucker standing in front of him what he thought. Bill said that he liked them and pointed to a couple of the caps and told him that he wanted those particular two. The man explained that he only sold them by the case and still thinking he was talking to the owner of the store he asked why he only wanted two. Bill told him that he needed one to spit in and one to cover it up. The hat man quickly packed up to leave and Ben and Glendel never knew about the near sale in the front of the store that day. The station was torn down many years ago and a Hess gas and convenience mart is there now.

Murphy Brothers was his stopping place around noon. Wilbur and Walter had a store on the north side of Queen and down from Gordon street. They sold electronics and furniture there. Walter loved to take a nap after lunch and let Bill watch the store so he could slip to the back and catch a few winks. Bill sat in a rocking chair up front and watched out for customers. If one came in he would tell his beloved jokes. Have you had a good job lately, he might ask? He would then proceed to jab them in the side with his index finger. They had then been jobbed. How many pennies in a dime? None. He would laugh. How do you call a duck in Japan? You call them real loud he would say. He would stall for time to allow Walter his forty winks.

Bill stopped in nearly every downtown store on those daily walks. One day he had just entered into the Sport Shop that I owned as the phone was ringing. It was a man from somewhere in California and he was selling light bulbs. I told him to hold on and I would get my purchasing agent. I handed the phone to Bill and said the call was for him. Bill was a very patient man and he listened most intently. It took about five minutes but the caller finally hung up. I do not know what Bill told him and I never asked.

My retired father was also on his stop of visits. Our family home was on McRae and next to the Methodist church. He and my dad created an imaginary business of raising birds for food. This was two men that had the most enjoyment out of something that did not even exist. Bill said his birds were called Mugwumps. He explained that they were so named because they sat on a fence with their mug on one side and the wump on the other. He bragged that they were very popular because they were so good to eat. My dad called his Mileimo birds. They talked about the large farms the birds required and the eighteen wheelers needed for this make believe business venture. My dad loved to carry on foolishness and he seemed to have met his match in Bill Tucker.

Bill did eventually begin his own small business. He made objects from wood he found around his home. He could often be seen with a collection of them for sale by the side of the road at Tucker Brothers. Most of the items only cost about fifty cents and no more than a dollar. I wonder if any of them still survive. I would certainly hold on to it if I had one. I just would. I thought of him the other day as the sun came up. Did you hear that? I remember him saying so many times. No. What was it I would ask? It's day breaking, he would say, and then poke my shoulder and laugh. I can still hear that laugh in my head. Bill died on the 25th day of April in 1999.

Chapter Twenty One

CONRAD HART

I watched the town grow with each passing year. It was the people who gave it life though. They enriched me and I recall them with great satisfaction. So many are gone now. I think of them often. Conrad was a native of Grifton. Son of Maggie and Thad Hart. They had a big house on Main Street back in the day. Conrad's first job was with the dry cleaners that Cecil Cobb and myself opened in 1949. Folks just didn't have the means to get into town to get to the cleaners then. Dry cleaning trucks would have routes into the rural areas to pick up clothes that needed to be cleaned.

Conrad had one of these routes. He had his own paneled truck and he serviced some very well to do families in Lenoir County. His customers liked him and gave him their business. He was very successful at his job. He paid a fee to have the clothes cleaned. A two piece suit cost seventy five cents. Gasoline in those days was an average of twenty five cents per gallon. Conrad was single and still lived at home so it averaged out to be a good income for him.

There were four of us at the cleaners that were about

the same age. J.R. Hooten, Snap Mumford, Conrad, and myself. We were all good friends but quite immature and loved playing tricks on each other. Conrad was the brunt of a lot of our joking around. He was good natured but a bit of a hypochondriac. He always complained of his stomach hurting or some other ailment of the day. We would tell him it was his imagination. Quick to tell him there was nothing wrong with him in spite of his insistence otherwise.

One summer the health department sent roving X-Ray buses to small communities such as ours and offered the test free to the citizens. Anyone could get an X-Ray without charge. Transportation was limited in those days and folks did not seek health care without an extreme emergency. This was considered a way of ridding disease and sickness before it started or spread. A bus came to us and most of Grifton took advantage of this opportunity. The results would be sent directly to the individual by mail. We four at the cleaners decided to line up and board the bus for the screening. Three of the four of us got a letter in about a week. It stated that they were happy to inform us that our test proved negative and our lungs appeared to be in good condition. Poor Conrad did not get his letter and really begun to sweat about it.

It was wrong. So wrong. What we did as he waited. I remember that we could not help ourselves. We devised a plan. A wicked one. We used one of the Health Department envelopes that had come to us and put a sticker on it with Conrad's name. We devised a letter.

Dear Mr. Hart.

We regret to have to tell you that your X-Ray was abnormal. One of your lungs appear to be eaten away entirely. The other lung shows large masses. Lower portions of the X-Ray picture masses in your stomach which are probably ulcers.

We urge you to contact your doctor immediately.

Signed
The Pitt County Health department

We waited with baited breath for Conrad to get the letter. He came into the cleaners one day and was grey faced. We knew he had received the ill fated and false news of his probable demise. He walked instantly in my direction and reached my counter looking me straight in the eye. My imagination? He taunted. Just read this! He said as he thrust the letter toward me. I took the letter and tried to be sympathetic but holding back laughter instead.

Then he told me he had to take some time off to attend to this serious health matter. We guys looked at each other rather sheepishly. It was then that we decided we had better fess up to our friend and admit what we had done. Conrad was furious and told us just what he thought of each of us. Several times. In looking back I know that it was a well deserved cussing out. He did forgive us eventually. I think he also slowed down on complaining about his health. His letter eventually came stating that his testing was normal. He even remained my good friend after that. We both finished growing up and now he is gone. He really did get sick and death finally took him many long years down the road. He got a real letter. That demanded his leaving us all. I miss him.

Chapter Twenty Two

ALF COWARD

The mark of his life remains indelible in our little town. Alf Coward was born in the Lenoir County side of Grifton during the mid 1800s. Records say it was 1864. He did not have much formal education. He was born in a time when most folks had to stop schooling early to earn money to live. Alf often found ways to make a living. He was definitely smart that way.

He found employment with the J. R. Harvey company early in his life. He once went to the owner of the general mercantile and stated that he needed a raise. Mr. John Harvey peered at him, a little taken aback, and informed him that he might not could pay more than he presently paid. Alf thought for a minute and decided that he supposed he would keep working for what Mr. Harvey was currently paying him. He knew he was faring well. The Harvey family always looked out for Alf. The Company was his main source of income although Alf could always find ways to supplement those wages.

He was friendly to everyone and spoke to all he met in

passing. He especially loved to stop and talk to the children of the town. They were all drawn to Alf who dressed in a white shirt with a tie. He wore a grey fedora atop his head. It set him apart and was what he was wearing each time I saw him. In cooler weather he wore a button up sweater over his shirt.

He was believed to have the powers to remove warts from hands or arms. At least he believed it. This was in the time before a wart was known to be caused by a virus and thought to be more mystical. He had his own ritual of removal. He would pull a blade of grass and rub it across the wart and all the while he would mumble, or chant, a few unintelligible words. This practice was handed down to him from past generations. There are those still alive in Grifton today that had warts talked off by Alf. He was often paid for that service which added to his income.

There are also those of us still living who remember that he whitewashed trees. Grifton had majestic oaks that lined most of the streets. The town residents had planted them to help beautify the community and they did. At some point someone decided they would look good if the trunks were whitewashed. No one remembers who started the trend but Alf was the man to hire to make it happen. He could often be seen pushing a wheelbarrow with a broom sticking up from it. Lime and water filled it and gave the look of being painted white when applied. The tree owners would pay him twenty five cents to paint the trees on their property. He would paint from the roots and upward with the broom and to about five feet high. Soon, all the trees of our town were uniformly whitewashed. The effect would last about a year.

Alf is buried in the cemetery on the road to Tick Bite. Turn where old Gower's store was located and it is past the railroad tracks and on the left at the sharp curve. The grave is easily located by the headstone there. The Harvey family made sure Alf had a fine one. The stone is an upright spire with his name, birth date, and the date of his death. Inscribed in granite are the words that he was beloved by all. Unfortunately, the cemetery is in a low spot and next to the Contentnea Creek. His grave was washed out during the heavy rains of the great flood in the area. The soft dirt washed away and Alf and his casket floated to the surface. It was tied to a tree to keep it from floating away and necessitated being buried a second time.

Alf Coward has a place in the history of the town of Grifton. I record his story to make sure he is not forgotten. He belongs in the telling of the town.

Chapter Twenty Three

ED RUTLEDGE

He lived in a true shack. Made of tin and located at Jolly Ole Field by the bank of the Contentnea Creek. Located just below what is now known as Gaskin's Landing on land that belongs to the heirs of the J.R. Harvey family from Grifton. I guessed the shanty to be about twelve by twelve and perhaps seven feet tall. Erected from scrap material he had picked up along the way. It had just one door and it faced the creek slough. The creek was important to Ed Rutledge. It sustained him. He had also lived in a hut at Pitchkettle on the Neuse River but I never saw that location.

I visited him often at his little makeshift cabin by the Contentnea Creek. It was outfitted very sparsely. It had one bunk bed and a 55 gallon metal barrel that he used to heat the place in winter. He also used it to cook and the air was often filled with the aroma of a good fish stew. I think I remember one chair in the place. Ed loved the creek and the surrounding woods. He knew it like the back of his hand. He could have walked through it blindfolded and never got lost. He knew it so well that he could go deep into the woods hunting and could recognize certain trees that told him exactly where he was and how to get back. He did not need to rely on a compass.

The Tuscarora Indians had once roamed the land long before Ed but he could have fit right in with them. Living completely off the grid the place had no running water, electricity, or any other modern amenity. He did not drive and had no means of transportation. He walked everywhere he went unless someone in the area stopped to give him a ride. The road leading to the creek was dirt and needed occasional smoothing and he would walk after the grader had come through and pick up Indian artifacts that had been uncovered. I owned the Sport Shop in town and he would bring them to me and I would give him a little change for them. They are now on display in the Grifton Museum.

Some people called Ed Rutledge a hermit. A recluse even. I don't think he was either. He was friendly and liked by most everyone. He simply chose a lifestyle that he liked and it suited him well. One particular cold winter a snow storm came through our area. The road to the shack was impassable for about three days. My wife, Edna, and I became concerned for Ed's welfare. We packed up some apples and oranges and carried them to him as soon as we could make our way there. When we arrived to the shack he had a nice fire roaring in the barrel and the temperature inside felt about ninety degrees. He had been more comfortable than the area residents who had lost electricity for days.

I believed it odd that there was no smoke inside the shack on that day from the fire in that barrel. You would have thought the air would have been full and I questioned Ed about it. He told me of a certain wood that would burn without smoke. The man certainly had all he needed. He also had no utility or water bill. He had no taxes to pay and had to spend very little on food. He seemed to have no worries. I guess a man like that slept well at night.

His death was as inconspicuous as his life had been. He developed a cancerous brain tumor and spent some time at a VA hospital in Virginia. He ended up at the rest home in our Grifton where he died. I only know of a couple of his relatives in the Hugo area. Even now, and every once in a while, his name will be mentioned by those of us who remember him. I always will.

Chapter Twenty Four

HOOK, LINE, AND SHAD

He unwittingly started an industry and died before he knew it. I cannot write a trail of stories about Grifton without a path leading to him. William Manning lived in the area and helped put us on the map. Most small southern towns have festivals to celebrate. Our town honors the shad. A fish that he helped bring to the surface of the waters of our local creek. It is one of the longest running festivals in the great state of North Carolina. The Shad Festival. My town honors a bony fish.

Shad and herring are not new. They have been in existence since the beginning of time. They have several members of the family. Nanny, hickory, white, and herring. They are all silver in color and indeed quite bony. Shad are anadromous, meaning they spend their adult lives out in larger waters but come up the creek in the spring of the year to spawn. They have always been a great source of food. Indians depended on the tasty fish for their food supply. So did the early settlers that landed by the banks of the Contentnea. There have been many shad fish fried right by the water's edge since then. Not much taste better than a fresh caught shad stew cooked in a cast iron pot as soon as the nets were pulled in. Nets were the early known method of catching them.

William Manning changed that. He was an avid fisherman. His love for it ran deep and I believe it was in his DNA. He was a good customer of mine when I owned the Sport Shop. He purchased his outboard motor from me and most of his tackle. His preferred catch was striped bass or rockfish as some call it. I also had the privilege of fishing with him on many occasions and it was an honor to do so. He wasn't much on patience though. Once we trolled for rockfish near Little Washington and I got hung up on the bottom. He stopped for me to get straightened out but my lure was hung up pretty bad. After a few minutes he asked me what test line I was using. I answered that it was a twelve pound. He sarcastically told me to give it a fourteen pound jerk so we could get back to what we came for. My friend was there to fish and not wait on me.

He fished about every day. Once he traveled to Washington D.C. on vacation and checked out boat landings up and down the Potomac while there. It was the spring time of the year. Many fishermen were successfully bringing up white shad. The fact that they were using hook and line intrigued him. He had only seen them caught by net. He questioned the anglers he met and observed their gear. Armed with this new found knowledge he perused the area tackle shops and brought home some of the bait he discovered there. He was excited to try it in our local waters.

Armed with his new gear he decided to first experiment with the waters at Pitch Kettle. That is a tributary of the Neuse River and known as an area for good shad catching. This was in the sixties and it was the first known try with something other than a net. No one in our area had tried a hook and line before. His expectation was to catch white shad as he had witnessed up north. It was to his surprise that he pulled up hickory shad. One after the other. He came away with a good haul and caught the attention of the other fishermen. Word of his method and catch spread fast. Shad were caught with this new technique all along the banks of our waters after this. You can now catch them from the shore with a hook and line and do not need a boat. He is believed to have been the first in our area to fish for shad. He had no idea what would follow with that fish.

The shad takes center stage each spring in this small town of Grifton. Since 1971 a whopping party is thrown in honor of that catch. In every way imaginable. There is the first catch competition which celebrates the first one caught in age and gender divisions. We lie about them in the Fishy Tales Contest. We even throw them in the Fish Toss Contest. We eat them fried and in stews with eggs and onions and it is almost as mouth watering as that eaten by the creek bank. In 1974 someone spray painted the words, Eat Mo Shad, on the drawbridge that spanned the creek. The words of that graffiti have been the motto of the event in the years since. William Manning would be shocked if he could see what he started at the Grifton Shad Festival each spring.

The idea of the festival did not begin with Mr. Manning.

The town wanted an annual celebration to bring attention to Grifton. Much deserved credit has been given to, Janet Haseley, who tirelessly worked to take it from just a dream to a day marked annually on the calendar. Shad fishing has become an industry in itself. Tackle shops sell the needed equipment and people buy boats designed for shad fishing. Gaskins Landing on the Contentnea has installed piers and the hickory can be pulled right to the banks. The season begins in the early spring with the best time being in late February to March. It is a favorite season with area anglers. William Manning should not be forgotten and I pen his name here among these pages. It certainly belongs in our town history. He belongs.

Chapter Twenty Five

THE VIEWING

We take respecting the dead to great lengths in the south. Especially in a small town like Grifton. Where everybody knew everyone. There was one funeral procession that is still mentioned from time to time. All the stops were pulled out for it. It took place in 1967. It took dignity to a new level. All the way down.

Tommy Sugg is my brother and loves a prank even better than me. His reputation is forever tarnished by some of the stunts he pulled in his younger days. A lot of the town graffiti could be traced back to him. He even bought a hearse to aid him in his deeds. A nearby funeral home upgraded and my brother bought their old one. My brother drove a hearse. It was long and black with side windows for better viewing of the many caskets it had hauled in the years before he owned it. It was loaded with chrome all around. It looked like a tank. He drove it with no shame. He and his buddies loved riding around in it. They took it to other towns to show it off. It took cruising to a whole different meaning. It got the attention they sought.

It started with a litter of young pigs. They had gotten loose from somewhere and were found roaming around the town. A friend of my brother herded them with his car to Tommy's house. They hastily worked together and made a makeshift pen suitable to hold them all. They knew the animals belonged to some farmer but had no idea who. He did the right thing and reported it to the Grifton police. The police was not equipped to handle swine. Not the four legged kind. They told Tommy to advertise around town. Put up some posters in visible spots. The officer told my brother to give it two weeks and if no one claimed ownership then the pigs were his to do whatever he wanted to do with them.

Tommy and his friends had planned a southern barbecued pig picking for quite some time. They had not been able to get enough money together to buy a hog large enough to feed them all. He eyed the new pigs and realized they were much too small to cook. He knew that if no one claimed them they were his to sell. There would be more than enough money to have a big throw down party with the price they would bring. He would not go back on his word though and set about making card board posters. There were just two. One was placed on top of the water tower high above town. The other was tacked onto a tree deep in the woods at Gaskins Landing. He waited the two weeks for the owner to step forward.

The grace period ended and no one had come to claim the pigs. No surprise there. Tommy now owned the drove. He promptly sold them off and counted his cash. Plans for the barbecue were set in high gear. A date was set. The friends bought a good sized pig with the money earned from the sale. Bobby Spikes rode with Tommy to Goldsboro on the day before the hog funeral. They purchased a keg of beer. It would be a good send off. They were so grateful they decided to really pay respect to the hog. He would be the guest of honor and center of attention. They dressed him in a white shirt and tied a tie around his fat neck. Pall bearers were chosen. Billy Burney, Wally Pittman, Tommy Humphrey, and Larry Benson served with my brother. They placed him on a cot and put him in the back of the hearse. He was elevated at just the right height so those passing could get a good viewing of the dead.

There would be a funeral procession on the way to the site of the celebration. Seven cars were filled with the party going mourners. They put on their best fake somber faces as they met at the edge of town. The line of cars began to head east at about Jigger Hart's house. Each car had their headlights on as is customary for a funeral in the south. The vehicles drove ceremoniously slow down Queen Street. Jean Williams and her sister, Murle Nelson, were pillars of the Grifton community. They were driving and met the oncoming cars. They immediately pulled off and waited for the line of mourners to pass. This is considered respect and dignity to honor the one gone. The two sisters were quite noble as the dead passed them. It was quite a shock when they glanced into the windows of the passing hearse. Miss Jean would later write about this in the local paper. The day she pulled over for a deceased hog.

The pig was roasted. The guys toasted it also. It takes several hours to cook a whole pig and so they had plenty of time to toast it again and again. They were no longer somber. Nor were they sober. I was told it was a fine wake and repast. An excellent laying out there on the coals. Like none had ever seen before. The hearse is long gone. My brother has settled down somewhat over the years. The dead is still talked about from time to time. I know of no other hog that had such a send off as this one in our small town.

Chapter Twenty Six

SMALL TOWN BOY

I watched the small town of Grifton grow up just as it watched me. In 1935 there were none of the modern day distractions that kept me from enjoying being a boy and enjoying childhood wide open. I do not recall that anyone knew anything about being politically correct either. One made their own fun and it just waited to be easily accessed. A doodle bug gave hours of fascination.

I never learned exactly the purpose of a doodle bug. I just remember loving to hunt for them. Most southern houses were built high off the ground and a child could stand underneath them. It was a grand place to play hide and seek near dark. The ground there was dotted with small holes about the size of a straw opening and indicated where the doodlebugs lived. They were a worm like creature with a flat head and little hooked cow horns. I loved to fish for them by making a mud pie and placing a dab on a blade of grass. I would dangle the stem down his hole and move it up and down to draw attention. There was always the accompanying chant, Doodle bug, doodle bug, come out, come out. It is suppertime. This was our early version of rap.

Bats often filled the summer sky at evening. They came from their day sleep to feed on insects. It was captivating to watch them fly fast and swerve down to catch their food. We took a straw broom from the kitchen and into the yard to swing at them. Hoping to knock them from the air. The bat has great radar and we rarely got one. We had hope though. We learned to hope.

The south is also an intricate maze of water filled ditches. A child and a ditch is a magical match. Not much was more fun than hunting for tadpoles. The water would be full of them after a nice soaking afternoon rain with the water often reaching up to our knees. It provided a good place to spend a hot humid day. Three or four of us boys would wade in bare feet and catch tadpoles. We often would cook them in a tin can over an open fire. It proved fun play but I do not believe I ever actually ate a tadpole. Never felt hungry enough.

Most boys got air rifles when they were about ten years old. I do not recall girls getting them in those years. You had a choice of lead or steel shot for the ammunition. I chose steel as the best and it cost about five cents a box. Most anything crawling or flying became a target for a boy and his gun. I loved to shoot lizards. Me and my friends would walk along the rail road tracks looking for them. They seemed plentiful on the cross ties and were an easy target. We did not bother cooking them but rather left them where they were.

Most any kind of bird became a target for us. My uncle

had a sawmill with a kiln that dried green lumber. Wes Pitt was the man that fired it. He roasted every bird we cleaned. He would tie a string to the leg of the bird and drape them over the fire to cook. He loved to join us for a taste of the wild feast when done. Sparrows were especially tasty.

Boredom was rare. There was no time for it. Fun stared you right in the face and was yours for the taking. Rainy days were more challenging for an outsider like myself. On those days I would just sit on the porch swing and watch the town before me as it became quiet and still while God did His work. I sat wishing God would hurry and waited for the sun to return. It was also a good time to find a secret spot to practice smoking. Grifton mapped in the heart of tobacco country. Our parents did forbid smoking so we had to hide. We did not use tobacco though. We used the weed called rabbit tobacco that grew in a field behind the town depot. We also used corn silk rolled up with a brown grocery store bag. We would smoke a cigar by just by making a fatter version.

We loved to play at school too. The swings and slides made us ready for marbles and jump boards. A jump board is closer to the ground than a see saw. One person jumped on his end of the board and that propelled the jumper on the opposite end. The object was to see just how high in the air you could go. It was dangerous and thrilling. I never see a jump board now. Most of us had bicycles but chose to walk to school instead and buses brought in those living outside the town. We used our bikes and roller skates in the paved streets. There were not many cars in those days and the streets were safe for use.

The local school also offered us a chance to play team sports like baseball, basketball, and track. In high school we often celebrated a birthday with a party. Spin the bottle was a popular game of choice. Everyone sat in a circle. Boy, girl. Boy, girl. A glass pop bottle rested in the middle and given a good spin. Plenty of time for me to pray that it would land on a girl that I liked because you had to kiss her on your turn. Sometimes, I really liked that game.

Grifton had the Contentnea. That beloved creek established a playground all its own. We went every chance our parents allowed. I loved to wade the water and fish. We did not own rods and reels but rather cane poles you could buy for about twenty five cents. It you could not afford that then you could cut down a wild reed that grew so profusely by the banks. The creek brimmed full of bass, perch, and catfish. It was good fishing.

Childhood got no better for me than those years growing up in our small community. The days when a child belonged to his parents, the school principle, and the teachers there. It felt so safe. I am satisfied with the raising it gave me. Fulfilled by it. Times sure have changed. I wish our children could go back to the days of the doodle bug. The days that were small town safe. I will leave this collection of my Grifton stories here for a record book. Maybe we could learn a thing or two. Just maybe we could.

Chapter Twenty Seven

Eastern North Carolina Fish Stew

Fish stews have been cooked by the banks of the Contentnea for a very long time. I thought it fitting to include my own recipe in the telling of Grifton. It has been handed down to me by my granddaddy, George Gardner. Has been tested over the years by experts which include my brother, Tommy Sugg, and my brother in law, Ed Reeves. This recipe is over one hundred years old. It must be followed as it is written here.

George's Fish Stew

*It must be cooked in a cast iron pot for best flavor.

Ingredients

2/3 lb. bacon
5 lbs. potatoes
5 lbs onions

5 lbs. of Fish
*Rock or striped bass is best.
Puppy drum or pond raised catfish would be next choice
Salt
Black Pepper
Red Pepper Flakes (For heat)
1 dozen eggs
water
*Tomato paste (Optional)

To Prepare

Fry the bacon in the pot. Take bacon out when done and put on a paper towel. Leave the grease in the pot. The bacon can be eaten as an appetizer while stew is being cooked. Turn the heat off the pot while other preparations are being made. This keeps the grease from burning.

Cut up the potatoes and the onions into chunks and put into separate containers. Cut up the fish into chunks.

Put a layer of onions in the pot.

Put a layer of potatoes next.

Add a layer of fish.

Sprinkle those layers with salt, black pepper, and red pepper to season.

Repeat each layer until you have almost reached the top of the pot.

Add water until it reaches one inch below the top layer.

*Add tomato paste at this time if desired

(Some like the taste of the tomato paste. I do not use it.)

Relight the burner at this point. Cook slowly until stew bubbles. Not a rolling boil. Never stir in the pot. This is important.

Cook about 45 minutes. The stew is ready when the potatoes are done. Test to make sure the seasoning is to desired taste.

Add eggs one at a time. Cook fifteen more minutes for them to get done.

Turn burner off. The stew is now ready to eat.

*Let one person dip the stew to serve. To ensure it is not stirred.

Writer's note:

This is a recipe for Fish stew as authentic as it comes. Enjoy sharing a pot with your friends. It's the only thing that can make it better.

Printed in the United States
By Bookmasters